The Garden Club 2

M.J. Sherman

Copyright © 2019 by M.J. Sherman

All rights reserved.

No part of this book may be reproduced in any form or by any electronic or mechanical means including information storage and retrieval systems, without permission in writing from the publisher.

Printed in the United States of America

First Printing December 2019

ISBN 978-1-64764-648-6 Paperback

Published by: Book Services
www.BookServices.us

Contents

Dedication v

Part One 1

Part Two 39

Dedication

To my granddaughter Hannah, who set me in the right direction. And to my husband, Mike, who always encourages me and keeps me on track.

Part One

Karen arrived before Gert and Mel. School, social activities, and part-time jobs had taken so much time that there had been little opportunity to meet at the clubhouse. Oh, they still spent much of their time together, just not at the old shed-turned-clubhouse. Now, missing their adventures in other dimensions, they had agreed to meet on this particular Saturday morning. Karen carried a stool outside and sat down to enjoy the early spring day, ripe with promise.

The wind ruffled the spring-green leaves and tickled the uncut orchard grass. A flash of red zipped past, and the *what-cheer* of a cardinal broke the silence. A phoebe announced its presence in the tree to her right. She looked for it in the enormous oak, but it was too well camouflaged amongst the green leaves. Then she looked up and smiled as she spotted the phoebe's nest tucked under the eaves of the clubhouse. Suddenly, to her left and very close, she heard a nasal chatter, *chickadee-dee-dee.* As she turned to look for the perky black-capped-bird, a fluttering at the corner of the big house caught her eye.

She forgot about the little bird.

What was that flutter? A bird? A mourning cloak, which was always the first butterfly to emerge in the spring? Maybe it was a leaf being swatted along by the wind. No, it was too large to be any of those; besides, it looked white. Like a curtain! *"But— but— the house is empty,"* she thought. How could there be an open window? There! She saw it again. It *was* a curtain!

"Should I go and see what it is? No, Karen, that's a bad idea. It could be dangerous. A hobo might have taken up residence. They sometimes move into unoccupied buildings."

She looked again. The curtain was not flapping out the window anymore!

The window must have been closed!

Now Karen was really spooked. She jumped up, grabbed the stool, and started toward the door. Just as she stepped on the threshold, she heard voices behind her and turned to see Mel and Gert. "Oh, good! You're here! I was afraid you weren't coming." She inhaled and let out a long breath. "What a relief!"

Gert and Mel looked at Karen, immediately worried because she looked pale and shaky. "Karen,

Part One

what's wrong?" Mel asked. "Yeah," added Gert, "What *is* wrong? You look like you've just seen a ghost." Still frightened, Karen snapped. "Well, if you're going to make fun of me, I'm leaving!

"Whoa." Gert held up her hands, palms outward. "We weren't making fun of you. We were just trying to lighten the mood a little. Please, sit back down and tell us what's wrong."

Mel put her hands on Karen's shoulders and after a quick hug, pushed her down onto the stool. "Now," she said, "start at the beginning."

Karen sat for a minute, trying to get her thoughts together. "Okay. You're probably going to think I'm crazy, but I swear, this is true!" Gert and Mel looked at each other, concern on their faces.

"I got here early, so I pulled a stool out here to enjoy the peace and quiet because the twin unit has been rowdier than usual lately, and I wanted to hear something other than their shrieky voices. I was looking around, and a movement over at the house caught my eye. I stepped down off the porch and started towards the house. As I got closer, I saw that what had caught my eye was a curtain fluttering in the wind! No one lives there, so how could there be an open window? And why isn't it fluttering now? The only possible answer is that someone is living in the house!"

Gert opened her mouth to answer Karen, but Mel jumped in before Gert could say anything. "Maybe

The Garden Club 2

the window is broken, and when the wind stopped blowing, the curtain quit fluttering around.

"But the wind is still blowing, and I don't see a curtain fluttering," Gert broke in. Mel gave her a stern look and a shake of her head. Gert shrugged her shoulders and looked questioningly back at Mel, which was exactly what Mel had been trying to avoid.

Karen saw the exchange between the two. She jumped up. "I knew you wouldn't believe me! I said you'd think I was crazy. The way you two looked at each other just now proves it." She turned and started down the steps toward the hole in the fence.

"No Karen. That look you saw was just me trying to keep Gert from making a smart comment, like she usually does. Please stay and talk to us."

Karen looked at her two best friends for a moment, grabbed the stool, pushed past Gert, and marched into the clubhouse. Mel and Gert paused for a moment, then followed her inside. Karen was sitting at the round table with the game box and the hourglass in front of her.

"Oh, good! Gert and I were just talking about the game. Gert opened her mouth to protest Mel's white lie. Mel shook her head and held up her hand to stop. Gert closed her mouth. Mel nodded at her and continued, "We thought it was about time to play again."

Part One

"Yeah," Gert replied, "can you believe it's been almost two years since we've had an adventure? I think we're about due for one. Let's get this game going. I'll bet one of you lands on a key. What do you say, Karen?"

Without a word, Karen reached for the box. Gert and Mel leaned forward to help her open it. "As to your question, Gert—no, I can't believe it's been two years since we've gone anywhere." Karen's mouth twitched slightly, then a hint of a smile whispered across her face. "I can't believe we're juniors in high school either. Let's set this thing up. I'd like to go on at least one more adventure before I'm too old to get there—wherever *there* is—and get back again!" They all laughed and began the game.

After playing several rounds of Huggermugger, they all sat back, their thoughts drifting to the subject that hung in the air—Karen's revelation about the curtain flapping in the wind.

"Okay, Karen, I have some questions about what you saw, or thought you saw. First, could it have been a piece of paper caught in the play of the wind? Second, might you have been slightly drowsy sitting there in the sun listening to the rhythm of the leaves rustling in the wind and the songs of the birds? Might you have seen a leaf floating around and just thought you had seen the curtain?" Gert looked directly into Karen's eyes as she spoke.

"No Gert. It was not a piece of paper or a leaf or anything else like that. It was too soft and billowy to be a piece of paper, and it was white. Have you ever seen a white leaf? I also thought about my being sort of dreamy, sitting there in the sun, but remember I told you that the cardinal had just flown past and startled me. I was totally awake and alert. I actually jumped and almost fell off the stool, it was so unexpected. Besides, I had already considered and discounted each of those things." Karen was beginning to get annoyed with Gert.

At this point Mel chimed in, "Well, let's walk over there and see if there's a chance that there might be an open window, or maybe a broken one. Maybe we'll find out something that will solve this riddle." She stood up and looked quizzically at the other two. "Inquiring minds want to know," she joked.

Karen mumbled something under her breath, and Gert was looking like she'd just been slapped. Mel really wanted to get out of there and break the tension. "Come on, Karen, Gert, we need to get out of here and clear our heads. Some fresh air will do us good." She turned and started towards the door. Gert and Karen sat for a moment, then stood and followed Mel out the door, all of them in a somber mood.

They headed across the lawn to the big house. Their steps slowed as they got closer. Finally they were standing at the corner of the house, close enough to the window to touch it. As they stood wondering what to do next, they heard a sound from inside the house:

Part One

a door being shut. Not slammed, but closed with an air of authority. Almost like a door that failed to catch unless it was made to do so with some force.

They turned abruptly and hurried back to the clubhouse. They wanted to run, but they weren't children anymore, and they were too proud to admit to each other that they were scared.

They reached the shed, unsure of what to do next. Gert was the first to move. She reached out and started picking up the brightly-colored glass ovals that were the pieces they moved around the board. The other two immediately joined in. They put the game back on its shelf, tidied up the rest of the place, and headed for the door. Not a single word was spoken the entire time.

Two days later they met again after school, determined not to let their fear get the better of them. Nothing was said about their previous meeting. They greeted each other, smiled rather stiffly, and entered the clubhouse.

Gert went straight to the shelf, pulled down the game box, and set it on the table. Mel and Karen pulled out their stools and sat down. Karen broke the awkward silence. "Well, lets get started. After all, this is why we came today."

After two rounds of play, Mel landed on a red key. "Oh good! I prefer the red cards. In case you didn't know, I *love* history. I wonder where we're going this time."

The Garden Club 2

"We don't need to guess. Just pick the darned card!" Gert growled.

"Well, I do believe Gert is either tired or angry. She only growls when she's in one of those two states," Mel teased with a twinkle in her eye.

"You're partly right, Mel," Karen replied," but I think she also does it just to get a rise out of us."

Gert listened to this exchange with a scowl on her face. "Okay, okay. Let's just get on with this. You two spend so much time talking that we tend to lose focus. My growling, as you call it, Karen, is the only way I can get you two back on track. Now, let's get this adventure started!"

Mel and Karen grinned at each other. Mel picked up the box of travel cards, pulled out the first red one and after a quick glance, exclaimed, "Oh, wow! We're going to New York City!"

The front of the card read "NEW YORK CITY, BROADWAY 1934."

She turned the card over. In contrast to previous cards, like the one for their adventure in Leadville, Colorado, there was no information or description on the back. "This isn't telling us anything except where and when." Mel sounded confused.

Karen reached over and held out her hand. Mel paused, wondering if the other two didn't believe her,

Part One

then passed the card to Karen, who flipped the card over several times. "Hmm," she murmured. "That's unusual. C'mon, Mel, turn this thing over, would you? I've always wanted to go to New York!"

Gert banged the hourglass down and motioned to Mel to take it. Mel grabbed the hourglass and turned it over. She pushed back her stool and stood up. Gert and Karen joined her. They walked to the door side by side. Karen opened the door and they stepped out—directly into a swirling, churning throng.

They were propelled half a block by the human current. Gert, on the inside of the trio, spotted a sidewalk cafe, pulled Mel and Karen out of the commotion and guided them to an empty table. Mel immediately collapsed onto a chair. Karen and Gert, after a slight pause to catch their breath, joined her at the table.

They had barely begun to get their bearings when a waiter appeared, slapped down the silverware in his left hand, dropped the menus into a jumble, and plunked water glasses in the center of the table. "Be right back," he said rather abruptly and disappeared into the restaurant.

The girls looked at each other and burst into laughter. After sips of water, they sat back and shook their heads at the frantic pace of New York City.

The water was cold and refreshing in the muggy heat. Karen said, "In geography class we learned that New York is the northernmost city with a subtropical

The Garden Club 2

climate." "Whew! I believe it," said Gert. Curious, they looked over the menus, then stood to leave. Mel dug into her backpack, found a quarter and examined it for a moment, inspecting the date. She smiled and dropped it on the table. She turned to the other two and said, "Okay, let's get this show on the road." Gert and Karen rolled their eyes and groaned. "What?" Mel asked, looking confused. Karen pointed to the street sign on the corner. It said "Broadway." Mel giggled, "I didn't even think about that! It's just something my dad always says when we're going somewhere."

Venturing back onto the sidewalk, they strolled along, looking into open doorways and shop windows, then turned onto West 46th Street to take a breather from the crowds. "Oh, look!" Gert exclaimed. "Isn't that the play you've talked about so much?" She pointed to a colorful poster in front of an off-Broadway theater. It said "Three Sisters, starring Beatrice Huntsman as Tiny."

"That's the one! Oh, I'd love to see it! Tiny, the eldest sister, is my favorite," said Mel, as she stood gazing at the picture of Beatrice Huntsman, thinking that the actress looked oddly familiar. The girls were discussing the impossibility of seeing the play, when a woman who had overhead their conversation approached. "Excuse me," she said. Mel turned to see the woman holding out three tickets. "I was going to turn these back in, but I'd like you girls to have them." She took another step towards Mel. Gert said, "Thank you, ma'am, but we can't buy them from you. We don't have the money."

Part One

"Did I say anything about selling them to you? I want you to take them and enjoy the show. Your friend here seemed so excited about the play. Here, take them and enjoy the evening." She grasped Gert's arm, put the three tickets into her hand, and folded Gert's fingers around them. Then she hailed a passing cab and disappeared.

The girls were speechless. Mel finally found her voice. "I can't believe that just happened."

"Me neither!" chorused her friends. "Let's go inside and see if we can get some information."

Not sure what to expect, they entered the lobby. Except for a workman mopping the floor, it was empty. A sign on the ticket window said, "Three Sisters: First show at 3:00 p.m." There was a list of ticket prices and a diagram of the theater.

They were looking for their seats on the diagram when the outer door opened and an attractive woman hurried into the lobby. She seemed surprised to see the girls as she turned to knock on the theater door. Mel broke away from her friends and approached the woman.

"Excuse me, but aren't you Beatrice Huntsman, the actress who plays Tiny? Mel could hardly get the words out; she was so awestruck. "Yes, that's me. And who are you? Do I know you?"

"I'm Mel—Mel O'Keefe; no, you don't know me, but I love this play and Tiny is my favorite character. I know the whole play by heart," she said, breathless from excitement.

"Well, Mel O'Keefe, it's a pleasure to meet you, but if I don't get to my dressing room soon, Karl will fire me. And you might have to take over for me." She banged on the door again. "I lost my key to the stage door, so I'm hoping there's someone here to let me in."

Just then, the door opened and a scowling man stepped aside and growled, "Well, Bea, I guess you misplaced your key again, eh?" Bea just nodded and slipped through the door.

Mel, feeling disappointed, turned back to Karen and Gert.

"Well, that went well!" Gert chuckled. Karen smacked Gert's arm. "That was mean, Gert. Don't you ever think before you open your mouth?" Gert looked down at the floor and mumbled something to herself. Karen grabbed Gert's arm, the one she had just punched, and pulled Gert toward the door.

It was just past noon, so they wandered off to explore New York until the play started. They walked through Central Park, then window-shopped on Fifth Avenue, stopping in awe in front of Tiffany's. They tiptoed quietly into the New York Public Library, then circled back to the theater by way of Macy's, where they laughed at the fashions of the 1930s.

Part One

During the play, Mel whispered, "Seeing the sights is okay, but none of them can hold a candle to this play."

Just before intermission, as Miss Huntsman was taking a bow, she spotted Mel again and smiled. When the curtain went down, Mel felt an irresistible urge to connect with the actress in person, so she excused herself as the girls were making their way to the lobby. "I'm sorry, Karen…Gert. My stomach is feeling a little iffy. I'll join you in the lobby in a few minutes." She hurried down the adjacent row of seats, already empty, hoping that the other two had bought her story. She headed directly toward the dressing rooms, intending to intercept the actress.

As soon as she stepped out from the group of actors milling about backstage, Bea saw Mel. *"There she is again! What is it about that young lady?"* She called out to Mel, "Hi— Oh, I'm sorry. I don't remember your name."

"I'm Mel, Mel O'Keefe, Miss Huntsman."

"Well, hello, Mel O'Keefe. To what do I owe this surprise visit?"

"I was hoping I could talk to you while you change for the second act. Or just sit and watch. That sounds kind of creepy, doesn't it? I'll leave now, before you have to call security." Mel turned and started down the hallway.

"Wait, Mel O'keefe. I'd love to have you stay and visit while I change. You can help me get ready. I don't know where Maria is. She's my assistant, but she's never here to assist me when I need her. Let's step into my dressing room and get going."

Mel was stunned. *"Bea Huntsman wants me to help her get ready for the next act!"* she thought excitedly.

Bea stepped behind a folding screen. "Please hand me that dress on the hook, Mel."

Mel carefully took the dress from the hook and handed it to Bea. Then she stopped, not knowing what to do next.

"Well! Don't just stand there, Mel. Help me into this thing!" As Mel stepped around the screen, Bea groaned. "Oh dear, I don't feel so good. Help me to the sofa, would you?" Bea almost stumbled; Mel jumped forward and grabbed her elbow. She escorted Bea to the couch and helped her lie down. A thick terrycloth robe hung on a second hook. She pulled it down and wrapped it around Bea.

Just then there was a knock at the door. The two women looked at each other for a moment, then Bea nodded to the screen and Mel ducked behind it. Bea said, "Who is it?" to which a very loud, gruff voice bellowed, "It's me, Karl. Were you expecting someone else?"

"No, of course not! Come in, Karl."

Part One

The man stepped through the door and stopped dead in his tracks. What ya doin' layin there? Why ain't you getting ready? And where's your assistant? You can't be sick. We'll lose the whole night's take!"

Bea thought fast. "No, it's okay, Karl. I only need you to extend the intermission another 15 minutes. I merely feel a little lightheaded. I'll be fine. I just need a few extra minutes. Thanks, Karl." As he turned to leave, Bea caught a slight movement out of the corner of her eye. "Oh, and would you do me a favor? When I came off stage there was a young girl whom I met earlier today. She was standing in the hallway looking like she might be sick. I tucked her into bed in the adjoining room. She came with two friends. Would you find them and tell them that their friend is not feeling well, that they shouldn't worry or come looking for her. I'll send someone to bring them here to join up with her after the play. Thank you, Karl. Well, don't just stand there; time's awasting."

Karl left to deliver Bea's message. Bea sighed, "I didn't think he'd ever leave. Now, will you help me on with this ugly dress?" Bea paused, then sank back onto the sofa. Oh no! I can't do this, I feel awful. Oh, Mel, what am I going to do? I don't think I can go back on stage!"

"Can't you just get the understudy to take your place?" Mel asked.

"No; she didn't show up tonight either! Oh, dear; Karl will be furious with me. What am I going to do?"

The Garden Club 2

She looked up to see Mel grinning, with a twinkle in her eye. "What? Tell me, Mel. Right now!"

Mel replied, "Do you remember our conversation in the lobby earlier today? You said I might have to take your place?" She stepped closer with the dress in her hand. "I could do it. I know the play by heart. I even know the songs." She broke into the first song, sung at the end of Act II, Scene One.

Bea looked at Mel in disbelief. "You sound just like me! Oh my gosh, Mel. This is the craziest thing I've ever heard of, but it might just work. Try on the dress. I'll button it for you. This is crazy! Oh, but you have a limp. What do we do about that?" Bea thought for a minute, then she said, "Just tell Karl you tripped and twisted your ankle. He'll make the announcement before the second act begins."

She shook her head and applied Mel's makeup. "When the play is over, come straight back here. I'll be dressed and ready. Just come in, put on your street clothes, and go through that door. There's a sofa in there and an afghan that you can pull over yourself. I'll send the girls in when they get here. Now scoot." She pushed Mel out the door. "Break a leg!"

Mel stood in the hallway, suffering a moment of panic, then shook it off and went to wait for her cue.

When the play was over, she rushed back to Bea's dressing room, washed the makeup off, and got into her street clothes. She dashed into the adjoining room.

Part One

She had just closed the door when Karl burst into the dressing room. Bea was sitting in front of the mirror removing her makeup.

"Well done, Beatrice! I don't think I've ever seen you give a performance like that before. You were at the top of your game tonight. Keep that up and you'll move up to Broadway in a heartbeat!"

Karl was louder and more exuberant than usual. Bea didn't know whether to be angry or proud. She thanked him and asked him to send in Mel's friends.

When Gert and Karen arrived at Bea's door, she invited them in and told them that Mel was in the adjoining room. As they moved off to see how Mel was feeling, Bea sat down and put her feet up. She closed her eyes and listened to the murmur of excited young voices. She felt a moment of annoyance, and then an inexplicable feeling of pride for Mel enveloped her. *"Why am I so proud of Mel?"* she thought. *"She just did what I haven't been able to do in my entire career: she impressed Karl. I don't think anyone has ever done that before. Mel reminds me so much of Bonnie— That's it! She reminds me of my little sister. I wonder where Bonnie is right now and if she's happy. I hope she finds a good man and rears lots of wonderful children."* At that thought Bea dozed off, a smile on her face and a tear in her eye. Just then the girls burst back into the room, all excited and nervous.

Bea reluctantly opened her eyes, smiled at them, and motioned them to a love seat opposite her chair.

"Just toss that clothing over the screen and make yourselves comfortable. Well, what did you think of the play? Was it worth coming all the way to New York to see?"

Gert was the first to respond. "Well, I thought it was wonderful. I can see why it's Mel's favorite. It's too bad she missed the second act. It was the best part of the whole play!"

"Karen, what did you think of it?"

"I agree with Gert. It was a wonderful performance. You made me feel like I knew Tiny personally. That especially came through in the second act."

A twinge of anger bit Bea so hard she had to catch her breath. *Well Beatrice, you asked.* Mel noticed the sharp intake of breath and raised her eyebrows in query, giving Bea a shy smile. "Come on, girls. We'd better be going. Bea has been more than helpful today, on top of performing in the best play ever. She looks tired. We should leave her to relax and recover."

As they reached the dressing room door, Bea called out to them, "Wait, why don't we meet somewhere for supper?" She was feeling a bit guilty about her anger at what Gert and Karen had said about the second act. "Let's meet at The Glass Hat at seven." The girls looked confused. "Oh, that's right, you're not from here. I'm sorry. It's in the Savoy Plaza Hotel at Fifth Avenue and 59th Street. If you get there before I do, tell Joe at the front desk that you're meeting me for supper."

Part One

She smiled, nodded, and closed her eyes. The girls hesitated for a moment; then Karen opened the door and they stepped out into the now empty hallway.

Since it was just five, they had two hours to kill before meeting Bea at The Glass Hat. They wandered around, looking in store windows and wondering aloud about the fashions that were popular at the time. They bought a bag of peanuts and sat on a park bench watching people pass by. At six thirty they hailed a cab and told the cab driver to take them to 59th and Fifth.

"You're going to the Savoy?"

"Yes sir, we are."

The cab driver chuckled. No one had ever called him "sir." It was always just "Hey, cabbie," so he politely answered, "Yes ma'am. I'll have you there in a jiffy."

They arrived at the Savoy early, found Joe at the front desk, and told him they were meeting Beatrice Huntsman. He nodded, smiled, and said "If you ladies will follow me, I will personally take you to Bea's table."

A waiter brought water and three menus. Gert smiled at him. "Thank you sir, but we will need another menu. We're meeting a friend here." He nodded, bowed, and walked off. A moment later he returned with the fourth menu. "Is there anything else I can get you ladies?"

Three voices chorused," No thank you,. We'll just wait for our friend."

Bea arrived at seven on the dot. She sat down and the waiter dashed over to the table with a drink in his hand,. "Beatrice, I didn't know you would be here tonight." He set the glass down in front of her. "Is there anything else I can bring you? Some appetizers on the house maybe?"

"No thank you, John. We'll just visit for a while. I'll let you know when we're ready to order."

"Okay, Beatrice, I'll be waiting for your signal."

After chatting awhile, they ordered their food. Mel said, "Bea you look like you're feeling better. I'm glad. I was worried about you."

John arrived with their plates. As he set them down, he said, "Bea, I didn't know you had a sister!" Mel looked up, startled, and started to deny it. Bea looked at Mel and shook her head. She said "Oh John! Don't be silly. These are just friends, one of whom bears a slight resemblance to me. Now girls, let's eat. I don't know about you, but I'm hungry."

After they had finished eating, they sat and talked for half an hour.

The four women rose and headed for the door. As they entered the foyer, a woman dashed up and grabbed Bea's arm. "Oh, Miss Huntsman," she gushed. "You

Part One

were just so wonderful today. I don't think I've enjoyed a play so much in a long time. I especially liked the second half of the play. You were magnificent!"

Bea shrugged the woman's hand off her arm. "Thank you, ma'am. I'm glad you enjoyed it. Now, if you'll excuse us, my friends and I are just leaving. Have a nice evening." "Oh, but Miss—

The four hurried out the door. Bea shook her head and muttered, "They think because they paid a few dollars for a ticket, they have the right to manhandle me and tell me what they think of me." Mel fell in beside Bea and whispered, "I'm sorry Bea. I shouldn't have pushed you to let me fill in for you. I didn't think about how it might affect you. I just wanted to see if I could do it."

Bea, surprised by Mel's apology, gathered the girl into her arms and said, in her best stage whisper, "Don't apologize, Mel. I'm the one who thought it was a good idea. I could have told you to go back out with your friends. But I wanted to believe that allowing you to replace me on stage would prove that I was a good person, and I would somehow end up being noticed and then invited to move up to Broadway. I know; it makes no sense, but I always thought I was this amazing actress who had to pay her dues by spending time in smaller theaters before moving up. It doesn't work that way for most people, but I thought I was one of the good ones. I'm just a mediocre actress with visions of grandeur. You are the great actress. You remind me so much of my sister Bonnie. I think that's why I went along with the crazy plan. I'd do anything for her."

When the girls heard the name Bonnie, they all gasped. Gert, in her usual speak first, think later mode, said, "Mel, isn't your mother's name Bonnie?" Just as she closed her mouth, the air around the girls shimmered and the girls vanished. Bea had turned away after her speech and was just turning back when she realized that they were gone. She was so stunned that she turned and stepped off the curb into the path of a bus.

∽

The girls reappeared just outside the shed with Gert and Karen facing Mel, just as they had been standing on the street outside The Glass Hat. Karen was the first to recover her wits. "Okay, Mel. What was that all about? What did Bea mean when she said you were the great actress?"

Mel looked at the other two, not sure how much she could, or should, tell them.

Gert barked, "Okay, Mel. Spit it out. What happened back there? It sounds like Bea was saying that you were a better actress than she was. Sounds like you weren't sick at all; you were just playing us for fools. C'mon, girl, 'fess up!"

Mel opened her mouth, closed it again, turned and walked into the shed. She plopped onto a stool and dropped her head into her hands. Her shoulders began to shake. Karen, the oldest of the three and the one most likely to fix things when they went wrong, stepped over to Mel, put her arms around her shoul-

Part One

ders and said, "Take your time and get it all out of your system. Then stop crying or laughing, or whatever it is that you're doing, and talk to us!"

Mel finally pulled herself together and began telling them about what happened in New York. When she had finished the whole story, Gert rolled her eyes, "You're telling us that it was you up there on that stage in Act II?"

"Yes, that was me up there! Do you want me to prove it?" Gert nodded, the expression on her face flickering between defiance, disbelief, and full-blown derision.

"Okay! I will!" Mel shouted. She proceeded to recite the last several lines that Tiny had spoken and sang the final song in a loud, clear voice. Gert and Karen were transfixed. As she sang the final notes, Mel turned to Gert, fire in her eyes. "There! Do you believe me now?" She turned and stormed out of the clubhouse. Karen dashed after her, grabbed Mel's arm, spun her around and hugged her so hard that Mel couldn't breathe. Gert stepped out of the door, took Mel by the shoulders, and turned her around. Then she did something very unlike Gert: she wrapped her arms around Mel and murmured, "Please forgive me, Mel. I had no idea that you could act like that. I really thought you were just telling us that story to make yourself look good. I'm ashamed of myself, and I want you to know that I will never doubt you again. How could I ever have thought that about you? Will you forgive me, Mel?"

The Garden Club 2

"How could I not forgive you? You and Karen are my best friends. I know that you weren't trying to be mean; you just didn't know that I knew that play as well as I did. I should have told you what I was doing. I was just going to talk to Bea for a couple of minutes, then meet you back in the lobby for intermission. You know the rest of the story. Now let's go back inside, or better yet, let's bring the stools out here and enjoy this beautiful day. All is forgiven."

Karen slipped inside and brought out three stools. They sat out in front of the clubhouse and soaked up the warmth of the day, listening to the birds and to the bees humming in the linden tree, which had just come into flower. Karen identified several birds by their songs, and Mel named a few as they zipped by. Gert, usually not one to do things spontaneously, hopped off her stool and plopped down on the cool green grass, plucking a tall blade and starting to chew on it. Karen and Mel looked at each other, burst out laughing, and joined Gert on the grass. They talked quietly about something, anything, and nothing for a while. After a few moments of silence, Karen asked the question that she and Gert had been pondering since their return.

"Mel, how did you know that play so well? How did you know the lyrics to all of the songs?" Mel thought for a moment and replied, "Do you remember, just after we formed The Garden Club, that we had one of our "cultural history" assemblies at school?" The girls nodded and waited for her to continue. "Well, that particular day featured a small troupe of actors who were here from England. They acted out a scene from *Three Sisters*.

Part One

"I was enamored with the play, and I wanted to talk to the actors after the performance. But I was on the planning and cleanup committee, and by the time I got done with everything, they were gone. When I made one last sweep of the backstage area, I found a copy of the script on the floor behind a chair. I looked around for someone to hand it off to, but everyone had gone already.

"So I took it home and put it in my desk drawer, and every time I had a few minutes, I would read the script. Eventually I had it memorized. That's my story and I'm sticking to it," she laughed.

Gert broke the silence. "Isn't it strange that the first adventure took us to Leadville just before we were assigned a history paper about a past event and now, the second adventure, Mel's, takes us to Broadway during the very short run of that particular play? As a matter of fact, I think there were just 23 performances, and we saw the last one." Mel gasped and looked scared. "Mel. What's wrong? You look upset."

"Or frightened, like you've seen a ghost," Karen added.

"I haven't seen a ghost, but I think I might know why there were only 23 performances of the play," Mel said in a tiny, shaky voice.

Gert was getting impatient. "Well, don't just sit there. Tell us why!"

Mel shook her head and said, "No, it's probably nothing."

Gert, having lost all patience with this narrative said, "Oh no you don't. You can't tell us you might know why and then say 'oh no, it's probably nothing.' Spill it, sister!"

Mel looked over at Karen who nodded her head and moved closer to Gert.

"Okay, here it is, and you'll probably tell me that I'm crazy. Just a split second before the air began to shimmer, I think I saw Bea turn and step off the curb into the street. I heard what sounded like brakes screeching, and then we were here. That's why I was so emotional when we arrived . I don't know what happened, but I'm afraid it wasn't anything good."

Karen jumped. "I heard that too, but I didn't think about it at the time. We were in the city. There are always brakes squealing and horns blaring. When we got back I was worried about you and forgot about it."

Gert, looking determined, said, "Okay, we've got a name, a place, and a date. Let's see if we can find any info. There's got to be something, somewhere. Let's go find it!" They returned the stools to the shed and walked in silence toward the fence and their bikes.

When Mel got home, she asked her mother if she had some free time to talk right then. "I have some questions I need to have answered." Her mother

Part One

nodded, put down the towel she had just folded, and motioned Mel to a chair. Mel shook her head, "No. There's too much commotion here. If you have time now, I really need your undivided attention." Bonnie felt a pang of worry. Mel was never one to need that kind of one-on-one. This must be something very serious.

"Okay dear. Your room or mine? Let's go now, before the hordes come searching for me."

They went to Mel's room. She sat on her bed and motioned for her mother to take the desk chair.

"All right, dear. What's on your mind?"

"Well, first of all, thanks for taking the time to talk with me. I know how busy this family keeps you. This could wait until another time if you need to see to the others." Bonnie shook her head. "No, you need my attention now and you'll have it. The others can just fend for themselves for a change."

Mel smiled, took a deep breath and proceeded. "Why do you never talk about your sister? She's part of my family, and I know nothing about her."

"Why the sudden interest, Mel? I know I haven't told you much about her. I didn't know that you were so interested."

We were talking about family trees and knowing who our ancestors were, and I realized that I know nothing about your family, other than that you have a brother, Uncle John, and an older sister. We see Uncle John often, but never your sister. I don't even know her name."

"Her name was Beatrice, and when I was ten, she went to New York to become an actress. My parents were horrified. A respectable young lady did not become an actress. That was a profession for girls with loose morals and low self-esteem. They forbade her to go. That was like waving a red flag in front of a bull. She became almost defiant after that, and one day she borrowed what allowance John and I had managed to save, took the cash Mom hid in the pantry, and left home in the middle of the night.

"Mom and Dad never mentioned her again. John and I sometimes wondered to each other where she was, but we never said anything about her when we were in the presence of our parents. I got letters from her for a time, but since I had no way to answer them, her letters eventually stopped arriving. That's the story of your Aunt Bea. I lost track of her. I got busy living my life, and she just faded from memory. Every once in a while something would happen and I'd remember the long-gone, adored older sister. Then my world would tap me on the shoulder and I'd get back to it."

Mel almost fell off the bed when her mother said Beatrice and New York and actress. Could it really have been her Aunt Bea that she had subbed for? Was it possible that she had actually met her? That she'd been hugged by Bea?

Part One

Bonnie noticed the shocked look on Mel's face when she had mentioned Bea's name, but Mel quickly recovered her composure and asked her next question.

"What happened to Bea? Did you ever see her again?"

"No, we never did. But late in 1934 we got a telegram from someone in New York telling us that Bea had died in an accident and that they would send her belongings to us soon. Eventually, we received a small package with a few things inside, including a necklace. I vaguely remember that in one her letters to me was a newspaper clipping in which she was wearing that necklace. How sad that was. All we had to remember her by were a few little trinkets and a playbill. There was an obituary from a local paper and a note from someone named Karl, I think."

Mel had to force herself to keep from jumping up and down on the bed. She had actually met, talked to, and been hugged by her Aunt Bea! Her emotions went from excitement to wonder to sadness and back to excitement. Her mother saw all of them flicker across Mel's face and wondered.

"Well dear, I certainly didn't expect that reaction. You look like you just discovered a long-lost friend and then lost them again."

"Oh well, I feel like I have. I've thought about her a lot—wondering what she looked like, where she might be, if I might meet her someday. I guess that will never happen, but I feel as though I know her better now. What did she look like? Was she as pretty as you? How did she sound when she talked? Could she sing like you do?"

"Bea looked and sounded just like you, and she was pretty. But you are beautiful. You could be a model. Don't get any ideas, daughter mine. When I hear you sing, she pops into my head. She was 10 years older than I, and I adored her, as younger sisters sometimes do.

"When you were born, I almost named you after her, but that would have been too painful, so I named you Mel and watched you turned into the exact image of my big sister. I always wished you could have met her. She would have loved you. You were like two peas in a pod." Bonnie stood, brushed down the front of her apron and asked, "Any more questions?"

Mel's reply was unexpected. "No. No more questions, but I feel like I've met her and that I would have loved her too. Thanks, Mom. Knowing more about her makes me feel better. I hope that wasn't too hard for you. I know that you miss her. Sometimes when I look up from what I'm doing, you're looking at me with a melancholy look in your eyes. I used to wonder if that look was because I had somehow disappointed you. Now I know that it was because you were reminded of your sister."

Bonnie gathered Mel into her arms. "Oh dear girl, I could never be disappointed in you. You make me

Part One

proud and happy, and I feel like I have a part of my dear sister back." Mother and daughter both had tears in their eyes now.

Bonnie strode across the room, opened the door, and turned to her daughter with a mixture of love and sorrow on her face: love for the beautiful daughter and sorrow for the long-lost but equally loved sister. She turned and stepped into the hallway, then stopped and turned back to Mel. "I just remembered; I have something I think you might want to look at. Come along, daughter."

They walked side by side down the hall to her mother's room. Bonnie waved Mel to the bed, then reached into a back corner of her closet and pulled out an ornate box covered in red silk, with gold and black embroidery covering the entire surface. "Bea sent this to me on my 12th birthday. I was so excited, but Mother was very unhappy about it. She said it was not a gift suitable for a 12-year-old, and she didn't want me to keep it. Thrilled with the present, I ran up to my room and plopped down on my bed. Should I open it or do as my mother wished and throw it away? I could not bring myself to throw it out. It was from my big sister!" Bonnie held the box to her heart as though it were made of gold and silver.

"It was the most elegant thing I had ever seen! I wanted to run downstairs and show it to everybody, but I knew that Mother would say it was gaudy and ugly and make me get rid of it. So I stayed in my room and put in it everything Bea had ever sent me, along with some of my own favorite things. I hid it away in my closet. I loved it, but I had no way to tell her. Then in 1934 we got the telegram informing us that she had died. When her belongings were sent to us, they were addressed to me. The package contained a necklace, a playbill from her last play, and a letter stating that all her belongings were to be sent to me."

She handed the box to Mel. It looked just like something that Beatrice Huntsman would have had sitting on her makeup table. The sudden stab of pain through the heart. The tears pooling in her eyes. The vision of Bea standing on the sidewalk outside of the Glass Hat. The screech of brakes. The blare of a horn. Mel dropped to the bed, sobbing uncontrollably. Bonnie sat down and gathered Mel into her arms. She rocked her daughter, talking softly to her until the weeping subsided.

"There, there, sweetie. Feeling better now?" Bonnie was worried about the intensity of Mel's reaction. Why did she react so strongly to the box? Maybe she was just upset about an aunt that she somehow felt close to. But Mel had never even met Bea. How could she be this upset over the death of someone she had never even known? She was a teenager, and they do tend to react strongly to the strangest things. Maybe this was just the latest item on a list of things that Mel had had on her plate lately.

Bonnie pulled some tissues out of a box on the nightstand and tucked them into her daughter's hand. She sat Mel back and searched her face for any

Part One

sign of another round of tears. She waited a moment and asked, "Are you all right now? Would you care to tell me about it, or should I just go and leave you alone for now?"

"N-n-no. Stay, please. I'm sorry about that. Something just suddenly hit me, and I couldn't accept it, but I'm over it now. For a minute, it felt like I had lost a piece of myself. Isn't that ridiculous? I've never even met her, and this whole thing was just more than I could handle. Why am I being so silly?"

"Oh, Mel. You're not being silly. You are a loving, caring person. I know that you've always been curious about Bea. I just wanted to wait to tell you about her until I thought you were ready. I guess I waited a bit too long. I do know that you always seemed to be searching for some knowledge of her."

Bonnie saw the startled look on Mel's face. "Yes dear, even among the commotion and chaos in this house I could see that you were looking for something. I saw you looking at the family pictures on the mantlepiece, and I saw that you recognized Bea, not as if you'd met her sometime and years later saw a picture of her and realized that you should know her, but as a part of yourself that had never been identified, a piece that you couldn't quite place.

"Now let's make you presentable. You put that box in your special, private place, wash your face with cold water, and come downstairs. The horde will be wondering where we are. Don't be surprised if they give

The Garden Club 2

you a hard time, assuming that you were in trouble. If you ignore them, they will get tired of pestering you and go find someone else to pick on. But why am I telling you that? You've already figured that out. See you in a few minutes, sweetie." With that, Bonnie closed the door and headed down to face the horde. Mel sat on the bed for a long time, staring at the box. She opened it, and a few more tears trickled down her face. There was the brush Bea had used while talking to Karl, and there, at the bottom of the box was the playbill. She took another ragged breath and hid the box in her closet.

∼

Mel arrived at the clubhouse before Gert and Karen. She was still sad after the session with her mother, but hiding behind the sadness was a flutter of excitement. Karen was the first one through the door, with Gert just a step behind her. She stopped when she saw Mel. Gert was so close behind that she actually knocked Karen forward several steps. "Oops, sorry Karen. Why'd you stop? I didn't expect you to stop so suddenly; what's wrong with Mel; she looks like she's been crying again."

"Don't ask me, Gert, ask her. That's why I stopped so suddenly. I was worried about her."

Mel looked at them, her eyes still watery. "Hi, I'm glad you're here. I need someone to talk to, and you're the two I chose. Will you let me tell you what I found out?"

Part One

Karen and Gert nodded in unison, looking rather like bobblehead dolls. Mel smirked. She waved them to the stools.

"Okay, here goes. I found out who Beatrice Huntsman is, or was." After a slight sniffle she continued, "She was my aunt, my mother's older sister. Mom said I look so much like her that it's almost scary." She continued with the story and concluded, "She got hit by a bus and died before they could get her to the hospital. What makes me sad is that I'll never see her or talk to her again. I only knew her for a few short hours. I think she saw us disappear and was so stunned that she stepped off the curb without realizing where she was. She never had a chance."

Gert jumped up, stumbled around the table and once again surprised the other two by grabbing Mel and wrapping her in a bear hug. After a moment, Mel relaxed into Gert's embrace. Gert was startled when she felt Mel go limp in her arms. Holding onto Mel's shoulders, she stepped back and said rather gruffly, "Okay, now start at the beginning and don't stop until you reach the end." So Mel told them them the whole story. "Remember when she said something about her younger sister Bonnie? I think that's the moment I knew, but I just couldn't believe it. I needed some proof."

Karen looked at Mel skeptically, "But her last name was Huntsman. Isn't that different from your mother's maiden name?"

"Huntsman was her stage name," Mel answered. Mom's last name, like Bea's, was Holtzman. I guess that doesn't roll off the tongue like Huntsman does."

Gert had been standing beside Mel during this exchange. "Well, at least you got a chance to meet her. You might have gone through life wondering what she was like. But now you have the satisfaction of remembering her. I know that doesn't make it any easier, but at least you have those sweet, wonderful memories to pull out and hold onto."

Karen and Mel looked at each other for a moment. Had Gert really said all that? It was so uncharacteristic. They had never heard her sound so caring and sympathetic before.

"Uh, thanks Gert," Mel stuttered, "that was sweet."

"Now don't go telling me that. I'm not sweet and I never have been. This just got the better of me and I slipped. Don't expect me to do that ever again! It was just a hitch in my gitalong." Mel and Karen burst out laughing. Gert looked disgusted and stormed out the door.

Part Two

After Gert stomped off, Mel and Karen sat down on a cushion of cool grass with their backs against a huge old oak. The breeze kissed their cheeks and ruffled their hair. They talked quietly for a few minutes, then fell silent. A bumblebee suddenly buzzed around their heads and shot off to a nearby bed of wildflowers, bobbing from one to the next. Mel watched the bee for a moment, then turned back to say something to Karen. She was startled when Karen reached over and clapped her hand over her mouth, shook her head in warning, and pointed to the big house. Mel gasped and nearly fell over. There a white curtain was gently fluttering in the breeze!

"See, I told you so!" Karen whispered. "Now you have to believe me. You've got proof that I wasn't just seeing things."

The Garden Club 2

Mel sat motionless beside Karen, not sure whether to stay and see if anything more happened or to run screaming to her bike. She shook her head and smiled weakly at Karen.

"You're right, Karen. I can't ever say that I doubt you or don't believe you again. Now, do we go over there and see what else we might find, or do we go home and pretend this never happened?"

"I don't know about you," Karen replied, "but I'm going home!" She stood, brushed off the seat of her pants, and headed for the fence and her bike.

"Wait for me!!" Mel squealed and dashed off after Karen.

∽

Their hunger for another adventure overcoming their fear, the three girls were back at the clubhouse the next Saturday morning. After two rounds of Huggermugger, followed by a short break, Mel declared, "Okay, we're going to play this thing until Karen gets her adventure! Let's roll up our sleeves and spin that dial."

Gert and Karen looked at Mel with amusement. "Ok, boss, you're in charge here." Gert handed the spinner to Mel, who spun it as hard as she could. "Ah…Mel? You won't get us there any sooner by spinning that thing harder." Karen chuckled, "Just take

Part Two

your normal spin and go, so I can take my turn. That's how we'll find out where and when."

After two more rounds, they were becoming frustrated and discouraged. Karen reached out to take the spinner. "I think this should be the last round if I don't land on a red key." She looked rather sad as she gave the arrow a lazy spin.

There was no red key in that round. It looked like they were finished for the day, so Karen reached out and started to gather the glass disks together. Gert stopped her. "No! We play until you get that key." Gert took her turn and handed the spinner to Mel, who reluctantly took her turn. She moved her glass disk and pushed the spinner to Karen, who looked at it as if it might bite her. Mel cleared her throat and pointed to the spinner. Karen reluctantly spun the arrow and moved her disk along the board...*onto a red key!*

"See, didn't I tell you?" Gert reached over, picked up the hourglass, and set it in front of Karen.

"Okay, Karen. What are you waiting for? Mel and I are ready for this, aren't you?"

Karen slowly pulled the front card from the box that Mel had pushed across the table. "Well?" Gert and Mel asked in unison.

"It says 'Chicago, 1871'." As she started to turn the card over, Mel asked, "Isn't that the year of the great Chicago fire?"

The Garden Club 2

"How'd you know that?" Gert asked.

"Because I listen in history class, unlike some people I know," Mel retorted, arching one eyebrow.

Karen read the back of the card aloud. "In 1871 a large swath of Chicago, approximately four miles long and one mile wide, was burned. The destruction included the business district. About three and a half square miles of the city burned between October 8th and October 10th. 300 people were reported killed, and an uncountable number were injured."

Looking up from the card, Karen asked, "Wasn't there a fire here in Wisconsin on the same day?"

"Yes there was." Mel replied. "It was in Peshtigo, a lumber town of 1,700 people in northern Wisconsin. They harvested white pines from the forests in the area."

"Was it a serious fire?" Gert asked.

Mel nodded. "Yes. It was the deadliest fire in recorded history in the United States. Over one million acres burned. The death toll was between 1,500 and 2,500. It burned many of the other small lumber towns in the surrounding area. But because Chicago was a major city, it got all the media attention."

Gert was impressed. "Wow, Mel, you really *do* listen in history class!"

Part Two

"Okay," said Karen. "Let's get back to the adventure. There's got to be a reason why we're being sent to Chicago, even if it was the lesser of the two fires. Are we ready? Should I turn this over now, or do you want to talk about the fire some more?" She had a tight grip on the hourglass, waiting for a reply.

"Go for it!" the other two chorused.

Karen flipped the hourglass over. The three girls stood up, Mel grabbed her back pack, and they stepped to the door.

"You can smell the smoke," Gert said and coughed twice. Karen opened the door slowly. The smell of smoke became stronger, and the air was hot. They stepped haltingly through the door and into total confusion. People and animals were wandering everywhere, obviously suffering from shock. Most didn't even notice the three girls standing in the middle of the road, dressed strangely and looking clean and fresh.

After a pause, the three headed toward the river.

Karen looked at the other two and asked, "Why are we going to the river? I can see boats still burning near the docks."

Mel turned to Karen and said, "The Chicago River is the link between the Great Lakes and the Mississippi River."

The Garden Club 2

"So what?" Karen asked. Mel looked at her for a moment, shook her head and said, "People head for water when there's a fire, and there's a lot of water here. They feel like they at least have a chance if they're near water; they feel safer by the river."

As they made their way to the river, they helped people as they could. Gert picked up a sheet, somehow still clean and white, and wrapped it around a woman carrying a small child. She wrapped the child into the folds of the sheet and then tied it around the woman. The woman never looked up or even acknowledged Gert. She was unaware of anything going on around her.

After walking through several blocks of smoke and soot, they saw a flimsy tent sagging in the aftermath of the rain that eventually helped put out the fire. They approached slowly, not knowing what they'd find.

What they found was a makeshift hospital, where three or four nuns and two doctors were attending to all manner of people. Some were families, some were lone children, some were women and men searching for children? Husbands? Wives? Many were either unaware or too weary to care where they were. A few cots and some sooty sheets and blankets were spread around on the ground. Some of the people wore bandages on parts of their bodies; others were obviously waiting to be treated. Babies cried; children whined or whimpered. Adults sat stunned, not sure what to do next.

Part Two

The nuns looked up as Gert, Mel, and Karen arrived. No one asked any questions; they just put the strong bodies and spare hands to work. A nun handed Gert a small boy, covered in soot and with his leg bandaged. "His mother is waiting over there." She pointed to a row of people sitting on blankets. "His name is Bobby."

The nun turned to help the next person waiting in line. Mel and Karen started tearing sheets into bandages. Karen whispered to Mel, got up and walked over to one of the nuns. "If there are buckets somewhere, my friend and I can go and get water." The nun pointed to the pails, bowls, and pots stacked up in a corner of the tent. Karen grabbed two pails, signaled Mel to help, and started toward the river. They hauled water back to the tent, poured it into the pots, and set them in a row along one side of the tent.

When all available containers were filled, Mel told one of the nuns that they would go out and see if they could find others in need of medical help. They snagged Gert on their way out of the tent. As they made their way along the charred ground, they saw an elderly man standing alone in the middle of the road. He didn't appear to have any injuries, but he was definitely in shock. Mel pulled out her water bottle and offered him a drink. When he didn't respond, she put the bottle in his hand and put it up to his mouth. After he drank a little, Gert took him gently by the arm and started off slowly in the direction of the medical tent. She took a couple of steps, turned and said, "I'll just see that he gets to the tent. I'll catch up with you when I'm done."

"What is it with Gert and crazy old men?" Mel asked, remembering their adventure in Leadville, where they had saved the life of an old man.

Karen tilted her head to one side, her eyes scrunched. "I think maybe she's fascinated by them. She never knew her grandfather, and her father left when she was quite young. I think she feels like she's connecting with the father figures she never had."

"That makes sense," Mel replied. "Now let's go find more people who need medical care." They wandered around for about an hour and then returned to the tent, where they were horrified to see the doctors and nuns using dirty cloths to clean wounds. Karen asked Mel and Gert if they thought that she could say something to the doctors without sounding arrogant. They discussed the plan and decided that instead of just saying something to the doctors, they would show them.

They gathered up empty buckets and headed for the river. As they walked out of the tent, they gathered up some of the older children and took them along. They explained to the youngsters what they were doing. Karen asked the older ones in the group to oversee the transfer of water to keep the necessary containers filled.

Part Two

After cleaning the rags as best they could, they all returned to the tent. The youngsters were excited to be helping. Some of them were so exuberant that they had to be settled down. Mel, having younger siblings, was elected to be in charge of directing their attention to the job at hand.

Gert found some bars of soap in a box of supplies. She set a bucket close to the small fire. When the water was just hot, she scraped a few chips off a bar and dropped them into the bucket, explaining to the young people watching her what she was doing and why. When the water started to bubble slightly, she poured some into a pot and carried it over to the table beside one of the doctors. She explained what she was doing to the nun assisting him. She picked up the used instruments and dropped them into the bucket. After a couple of minutes she fished them out with a wooden spoon that she found in the box of supplies and laid them on a clean square of cloth. She then filled a bowl with hot soapy water and set it beside the doctor. "To wash your hands in after working on a patient," she said quietly.

After organizing the youngsters into groups to keep the flow going, Mel, Karen, and Gert, needed to rest before returning to their search for injured people. They sat down under a tree that had miraculously escaped being burned. Gert, ever the pessimist, said, in what could only be described as a whiny voice, "I'm hungry, and I'm sure there's nowhere to find any food here. What do you geniuses suggest we do?"

The Garden Club 2

Mel picked up her backpack and pulled out some oranges, two apples, and a bag of potato chips. She handed them to Karen and Gert, who had the humility to look embarrassed. "Wow, Mel, you really are a genius. Thank you very much. I apologize. I have to learn to think before I open this big mouth." They ate the fruit, shared the chips, and each had a drink of water.

As they ate, Gert wondered aloud exactly what Chicago had looked like before and what it would look like after it was rebuilt. She began to draw in the soot beside her. Karen saw her and poked Mel, who had closed her eyes briefly. Mel jumped, looked at Karen and started to ask why she had poked her. Karen put her finger to her lips and pointed to Gert. The two watched, fascinated as a skyline appeared in the dirt beside Gert.

After a moment, Gert looked up and saw the other two watching her. She blushed and wiped the drawings with a stick she had found. Mel and Karen gasped and simultaneously cried out, "No Gert!" Mel said, "Don't erase that! It was amazing! What was it?"

Gert blushed and said, "It was just a stupid idea of what I thought Chicago could look like after it was rebuilt." The other two looked at her in awe. Karen said, "Gert, you're really good at that. You should become an architect!" Mel nodded in agreement.

They surveyed the area around them. The whole world was black and sooty, and the sky was obscured

Part Two

by tendrils of smoke still rising from the ruined city. They were looking out on a black-and-white world. They didn't like what they saw.

Finally they stood up and started off to look for more people. As they turned a corner, Karen stopped and put her hands out to stop the other two. "Did you hear that?" she asked. "It sounded like a child crying."

Gert, always the sceptic, said, "It's probably just a bird or a small animal. I doubt there would be any children still in this section."

"There it is again. Listen— There!" She pointed to her left. "That's definitely a child crying, and I'm going to find them!" She took off in the direction of the sound, Mel on her heels and Gert a step or two behind, all of them trying to pinpoint the exact location of the crying. They zeroed in on a barn. There were a couple of houses still standing nearby, but they determined that the crying was definitely coming from the barn.

Karen dashed ahead and pushed through the barn door. As she burst in, the crying stopped. By this time Mel and Gert had arrived. They began to search through the stalls and small rooms. They searched the tack room carefully. There were lots of places where a child could hide.

They returned to the main part of the barn. Gert tapped Karen on the shoulder and pointed up at the hayloft. She looked up and saw a pair of blue eyes and a pair of brown eyes peering down at her. "Hi. My name

The Garden Club 2

is Karen, and these are my friends Mel and Gert. What are your names?" There was no answer, but the brown eyes filled with tears, and the girls heard another muffled sob. Mel, thinking about her younger siblings, said softly, "It's okay; the fire is out; there are no more flames here. You're safe now."

The blue eyes closed for a moment, and then a blond head, a button nose, and a bow of a mouth emerged from the pile of hay.

A young child's voice broke the silence. "My name is Reginald Amadeus Beaufort the Third and I didn't cry and this is my best friend Esther Brown and she did cry but that's okay because she's a girl and girls cry about everything," the dimpled boy blurted out, all in one sentence, without taking a breath.

Karen turned around, her back to the ladder, trying not to laugh at the precocious boy. Mel chuckled, then coughed to cover the laugh. Gert also turned around, her shoulders shaking with laughter. Karen turned back, looked up at the hay, and discovered another face, this one with brown eyes and a mop of curly brown hair nearly as dark as Karen's. "Well, Reginald Beaufort and Esther Brown, would you care to climb down the ladder now?" Karen was still trying not to laugh out loud, when a voice said boldly, "I could have climbed down at any time but Essie was afraid, so I stayed up here with her and you forgot to say "the Third." It's Reginald Beaufort the Third."

Part Two

"I apologize, Reginald. I will remember to say "the Third" next time. Now, how about climbing down here?" The blue eyes scrunched closed, and the brown ones brimmed with tears.

"How about if I come up and help you down. My friends Mel and Gert will help too. Okay?" No answer from above, just a scuffling and a slight nod from the blond head. "Okay, I'm coming up. Could you both please move back so I can get up there with you?" The heads disappeared into the pile of hay as Karen chuckled and started up the ladder.

Gert followed Karen up halfway and leaned into the ladder for support. Mel stood at the bottom ready to receive the youngsters as they were handed down.

Karen reached the top and disappeared over the edge. Gert and Mel heard Karen's voice, then the excited voice of Reginald. The words weren't clear, but there was definitely a serious conversation going on in the loft.

"Hey, are you all coming down, or should we come up there and join the party?"

Karen leaned over the edge of the loft and scowled at Gert. "You need to learn to be more patient, Gert. I can't just grab these two and dangle them over the edge. I'm trying to build a little trust between us. If you can't hold on and want to climb back down, I'll let you know when we're ready, and you can climb back up here."

Gert shook her head and looked down at Mel, who just smirked and waited patiently. "Okay, who's first?" No answer. "How about you, Reginald Beaufort the Third? You seem like a brave boy."

"I-I-I could climb down by myself, b-b-but I'll let you help me, so Essie can see how we do it. Then she won't be scared."

Reginald took a tentative step toward the ladder. Karen held his hand as he neared the edge. "Why don't you turn around and go down backwards? Gert will be there to help you when you get down below my reach. Okay?"

He hesitated, contemplating the suggestion, then turned, looked at Esther, and nodded. The process went smoothly with Reginald, but Esther was not so sure about climbing down.

"How about if I climb down only partway," suggested Karen, seeing the panic in the brown eyes. Then you can put your arms around me. We can hold onto each other. Does that sound like a plan?" Esther thought about "the plan" for a moment, then nodded her head, dark brown curls bobbing up and down.

"Okay, you stand right here." Karen patted the hay beside her. Then she stood up, turned around, and stepped down one rung…two…three. Esther began to whimper as Karen appeared to go lower and lower. "It's okay, sweetheart; I just have to go down far enough so that I can get my arm around you." At this point

Part Two

Karen began to hum a song her grandmother sang to her when she was sad or afraid. Granny had told her it was a song her own nana sang to her. It was called "She Wore A Yellow Ribbon," and she sang it because Karen often wore a yellow ribbon in her hair.

"Look, Essie—may I call you Essie?—Gert is right there to help us down, and Reginald is waiting down there too." Karen paused for a moment. There was something so comforting and familiar about this sweet little girl. Something about her eyes and the slight downturn of her mouth made Karen hesitate again.

Finally, Esther reached out and wrapped her arms around Karen's neck.

"Not quite so tight, sweetie; you're choking me. Don't worry, I have hold of you, and Gert is right there to help us down." She lifted Esther up so her feet were off the floor, and the girl immediately tightened her grip. Karen started humming again, and Esther relaxed just enough so Karen could concentrate on moving down the ladder. Gert climbed up a couple of rungs and reached out to brace them. Gert stepped down two rungs, still with a hand on Karen's hip, then Karen stepped down. And so, rung by rung of the long ladder, they got Esther to the floor of the barn. Mel and Reginald were not there, but they could hear voices in the tack room.

"Now, young lady, let's go see if we can find that rascal Reginald." Gert took Esther's hand and started off toward the tack room. Esther looked back at Karen, a worried look in her brown eyes. "Don't worry about Karen, honey; she'll be all right; she just needs to sit a minute," Gert whispered to the little girl. Then she whispered something else, and a tiny smile appeared on Esther's face.

Karen sat down on a hay bale, her hands and knees shaking and her mouth dry. She looked around and saw Mel's backpack on the bale beside her. She reached over and dragged it to her side. It was almost more than she had the strength to do. She unzipped the pack and dug through it until she found the canteen that Mel always carried with her. Karen screwed off the top and upended canteen. The water was somehow still cold and refreshing. She put the canteen back, put her elbows on her knees, and dropped her head into her hands.

After what seemed like only a minute, she felt a hand on her back. She looked up to see Gert standing beside her, a grin on her face. "That was magnificent, my friend. You looked like a professional up there. I'm not sure I could have done that. I would have had to go find someone to get her down. What do you suppose they were doing in that loft? By the way, I am proud to call you friend. Oh, and I left the youngsters in Mel's capable hands. I wanted to check on you. You looked done in when we went to find Mel and Reginald."

Karen grinned at Gert. "The third—you forgot. It's Reginald Amadeus Beaufort the Third! I won't tell him you forgot," she teased. "That will be our little

Part Two

secret. Do you think Mel will mind that I dug through her backpack for her canteen?"

Gert's reply was a guffaw and a shake of her head. "I think she would have been more upset if you had waited because we would probably have found you passed out on in the hay if you hadn't had any water. I'm sure she would have done the same thing if the situation had been reversed. Now come here. You need a hug!" She pulled Karen to her feet and wrapped her arms around her. Karen's only response was a huge sigh.

Just then, Mel arrived, a child's hand in each of hers. "Here they are! I told you Karen hadn't gone away. She's right here where you left her." Esther let go of Mel's hand and took Karen's, a ghost of a smile on her face.

Leaving the barn, Reginald led them around a corner and down a dirt street. Esther was holding tightly to Karen's hand. Reginald broke free from Mel's hand and began dancing around, running ahead and circling back, his feet kicking up clouds of fine ash that had drifted into the neighborhood. Gert was getting annoyed by his antics. As he danced past her again, she reached out and grabbed him by the arm. He looked like he might protest, but she gave him what her friends jokingly called "the Gert look," and he stopped fidgeting immediately. She took him by the hand, and they walked the rest of the way quietly behind the other three.

Reginald glanced up at Gert and started to say something, but he paused, not sure if he should. Gert nodded okay and smiled at him. He pointed to two houses, off to the right. One was a large, stately brick house with a fenced yard and well-trimmed shrubbery.

A narrow dirt path led to the second house. It was small and slightly dilapidated. It had once been a bright buttery yellow, but the paint had faded over the years, flaking off in spots . The front porch sagged disconcertingly, as if a heavy weight on one side might tip the whole house over. The heavy vines climbing up the support posts struggled to hold up, or perhaps disguise, the drooping roof. A porch swing listed badly to one side, adding to the illusion that the building was losing its balance. In stark contrast, standing proudly along either side of the dirt path were several round metal tubs overflowing with a riotous array of flowers reaching out to shake hands with anyone who walked up to the house. A rainbow of zinnias, yellow calendulas, sweet Williams, pinks, and sweet alyssum disbursed their individual fragrances generously, the separate aromas mingling into a heady perfume as they fluttered gently in the late morning breeze. It was a wonderful surprise after the rancid stench of burned wood and wet ashes.

"That's Essie's house." Reginald pointed to the once-yellow bungalow. "And that's where I live," he explained as he turned and pointed to the imposing brick Victorian. "I like to play at Essie's house because it's more fun. We have lots of 'tiques at our house, and I'm not allowed to run around or even touch anything

Part Two

because Mother says I'll break them." Gert looked down at Reginald and shook her head. " 'tiques?" she asked, puzzled.

"You know—old stuff." Reginald replied.

"Oh, you mean *antiques*," Gert said and chuckled softly.

"Yes, and Father says I need to learn to be more careful, 'cause they're all going to be mine one day if I don't break them all." This time Gert laughed out loud. Mel and Karen turned around to see what had set her off. She just shook her head.

As the five of them neared the small house, the front door opened and a plump, brown-haired woman stepped out onto the porch. The screen door slammed behind her. She put her hands over her face, covering the tears that trickled down her cheeks.

"Here you are, you naughty, naughty children. Oh, I was so worried about you! The neighbors are all out looking for you. Where have you been? I was worried that you were trapped by the fire and holed up somewhere." She knelt down and pulled the two children to her breast. She looked up at Gert, Mel, and Karen. "Wherever did you find these two? I hope you didn't have any trouble with these rascals."

"No, ma'am, no trouble at all." Karen replied.

The Garden Club 2

"Ma'am? I'm not ma'am. I'm Olga—Olga Brown—and this is my daughter Esther, but I'm sure you know that by now. And this little scamp is Reginald Beaufort." As if one voice, the three girls said "the third," and they all burst out laughing.

"Please, come in and sit down. Let me just get these two settled, and you can tell me how you found them. Please! Sit and rest. You look tired." Olga hustled the children through the door. She returned several minutes later with three plates heaped with food. She set them on the worn tabletop and motioned to the girls. "You three look tired and hungry. I thought you could tell me all about finding those two while you are eating. Go ahead. Dig in."

The girls stared for a moment at plates heaped with warm slices of ham, freshly-baked biscuits, green beans with small pieces of bacon mixed in, and on the side, a container of gravy to pour over the biscuits. Olga then retrieved a freshly-baked blackberry pie from the pie safe and proceeded to transfer three enormous slices to small plates.

Gert didn't wait for the others. She stuck her fork into a piece of the warm glazed ham, took a bite, closed her eyes, and groaned with pleasure. Karen and Mel watched her and then dug into their own food. Their response was identical to Gert's. Olga smiled at their reaction. She knew hungry teenagers when she saw them.

Part Two

"Okay, now tell me where you found those two. I want the whole story, from the beginning to when you showed up at my door." Olga waited for a response.

The girls reluctantly put down their forks and stared at Olga for a moment. Karen spoke first, with Mel and Gert filling in details where needed. They got the whole story out, with some questions from Olga. When they reached the end, Olga sat still, not saying a word. She finally smiled and said, "Oh my! You young ladies have had a busy day. If you'd like to stay, I can fix up the porch for you. It's getting late, and it will soon be too dark to find your way back to the medical tent."

Gert answered before the others could even open their mouths. "Thank you so much, Mrs. Brown. You've been extremely kind, and the food was wonderful, but I think we really need to get back. When we left, the nuns all said to hurry back. They probably think we've abandoned them."

Olga frowned slightly, then nodded and stood up. "Please stay right there for a few minutes. I'm going to fix a basket of food for you to carry back with you. They probably haven't stopped to eat anything at all today. Why don't you say goodbye to the children while I fill the basket?"

The girls nodded and went through the kitchen out to the porch. Olga listened as the three girls told the youngsters that they had to leave. There was crying—it sounded like Essie—then some soft words and then

The Garden Club 2

laughter all around. "My, my! Those girls certainly have a way with children. I'll bet they all come from loving families," Olga said to herself.

The young people all trooped into the kitchen, Essie holding tightly to Karen's hand and Reginald walking between Mel and Gert, holding a hand of each.

Olga held out the laden basket, and Gert took it with her free hand. As she leaned in to grab the handles, Olga hugged her. After thanking Gert, she stepped up to Mel, thanked her, and gave her a hug. Finally, she gave Karen an extra long hug, thanked her, and asked her if she would give a message to Dr. Robert McCort. Karen nodded. "Please tell him that his things have been mended, and he can pick them up on his way home. Also I'll have boiled some coffee for him." She blushed and reached for the children's hands.

As they walked back toward the tent, Gert, in her inimitable way said, "Did you see Olga blush when she mentioned the good doctor? I think she has a thing for him."

"Gert, that's not respectful or nice!" Karen protested. "You always speak before you engage your brain!" "Try thinking before you speak!" Mel blurted out. They walked on in an uncomfortable silence. When they reached the tent, Mel handed over the basket of food to a grateful helper, and Karen asked the first nun she encountered to please point out Dr. McCort. The nun waved her hand toward the far side of the tent and went over to distribute the food.

Part Two

Karen wove her way through the tent and stopped in front of the doctor. He was sitting on a wooden box with his back against a support pole. His eyes were closed. Karen stood in front of him, trying to decide if he were asleep or not. Without opening his eyes he said, "Well, don't just stand there, who are you, and what do you want?" Karen cleared her throat and choked back a retort. "I have a message for you from Olga Brown."

One of the good doctor's eyes popped open. "How do you know Olga? Why would she give you a message for me? She usually comes down here herself." The eye closed again, and the gruff voice demanded, "Well?" Karen gritted her teeth and gave him a highly-edited version of the story they told Olga earlier, as well as her message to Dr. McCort. The ghost of a grin appeared on his mouth, the other eye opened, and then a highly audible chuckle rattled across the tent. The nuns all turned to look their way and immediately turned back to their food, repressing smiles.

"Those two scamps. They're always up to something, usually something they shouldn't be up to, and Reggie is usually the one in the lead. Are the children okay? Where did you find them? Did Olga feed you? Well, are you going to answer or just stand there with your mouth open?" Karen's response was as curt as the doctor's. She said, "Yes, in the Johanson's barn, and yes." She turned abruptly and strode off toward the other two girls. What a rude man! That was no way to talk to anyone! She was angry, and she was ready to leave.

The Garden Club 2

Mel and Gert were explaining where the basket had come from when they heard a harsh laugh from across the tent. Gert looked up, saw Karen marching toward them, and warned Mel that they should be ready for whatever happened when Karen arrived.

Karen stormed up, grabbed Gert and Mel by the arms and pulled them out of the tent. "Oh, that man! How could a doctor be so rude?"

Mel hung back for a couple of steps and fell in beside Karen. "What happened back there?" she asked. The air shimmered. Gert sidestepped suddenly, causing the other two to run into her. They toppled to the ground in a tangled heap and found themselves lying on the grass just beside the clubhouse door. "Oof!" "Ouch!" "Get off my leg!" While trying to untangle various arms and legs with all the squirming and wiggling going on, Karen put her hand down to steady herself. She felt something hard and cool and closed her hand around it. Standing up, she offered a hand to Gert. When Gert was upright and steady, they both reached down and pulled Mel to her feet. As the girls were helping her up, Mel caught sight of something in the grass. When she was steady on her feet, she reached down and wrestled a piece of wood out of the long grass that held it. It was the wooden sign that they had hung over the clubhouse door.

The Garden Club
Est. 1958
Gert   Mel   Karen

Part Two

"Oh! I didn't even notice that this was missing, did you?"

"No!" came the reply.

Karen held up her left hand, still in a fist. "I found something too." She opened her hand. Gert reached over, paused, and asked, "May I?" Karen nodded, and Gert took a flat round silver object out of Karen's hand. Gert examined it carefully. It was a silver dollar. They headed into the clubhouse and pulled one of the encyclopedias from the shelf. Mel opened it and began searching the index. "Ah, here it is. It's called the 'Seated Liberty,' minted in Philadelphia from 1840 to 1873. There were only a few thousand minted. How do you suppose it got here?"

"Isn't it odd that Karen found it beside the clubhouse just as we returned from an adventure to that time period?" Gert asked. They all agreed that it was indeed eerie, and they also agreed that they were very tired. They put away the game board and the hourglass and walked to their bikes.

When Karen got home, she found her mother in the kitchen. "Mom, can you spare a few minutes? I have a couple of questions for you—about Nana's mom."

"Of course, honey. I'll answer any question that I can. Shall we sit down? What would you like to know?"

"What was your grandmother's maiden name? I never thought to ask before."

"Well, she was born Esther Karen Brown, but she was adopted by her stepfather. His name was McCane or McCall—or something like that."

"Could it have been McCort?"

"Yes! That's it. Robert McCort. He adored Esther, spoiled her rotten."

Karen had stood up to get a glass of water. Stunned, she clutched the back of her chair for support, lest her sudden dizziness cause her to fall. *Oh my gosh, the little girl I carried out of the hay loft was my great grandmother! I wonder who Reginald Beaufort the Third was.*

"Sweetheart, I just asked you why the sudden interest in my grandmother's surname."

"Oh! Sorry, Mom. I just wandered off there for a moment. I'm asking because we were talking about family trees in history class, and I realized that I knew very little about her. Another question: Do you remember her, and did she ever sing to you when you were growing up?"

"Yes, of course I remember her. She was only in her fifties when I was born. Whenever I was scared or worried about something, she would rock me in an old wicker rocker and start humming a song. I don't

Part Two

think she even realized she was doing it. It was just what she did, and I found it very comforting."

"Do you know what the song was?"

"It was 'She Wore A Yellow Ribbon.' Why do you ask?"

"Mom, that's the song Grandma—that would be Esther's daughter and your mother, right?—that's the song Grandma used to sing to me. She said it was because you often put yellow ribbons in my hair. But she only did it when I was scared or worried."

At this point Karen was having trouble not jumping up and running to the phone. The whole thing was overwhelming. She couldn't wait to tell Mel and Gert! The only thing left to do was to find out where Reginald fit into all of this. Was he still alive? He would have to be in his nineties. Maybe she could enlist Gert and Karen. They were so good at research.

In the meantime, there were summer jobs to think about. She and Gert would be graduating next year, a year early, and Mel would be graduating the following year. It would be a year of endings and beginnings. Reginald would have to wait until winter break.

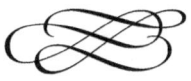

www.ingramcontent.com/pod-product-compliance
Lightning Source LLC
LaVergne TN
LVHW011740060526
838200LV00051B/3276